PACK PR

for all Cub Scou

compiled by
MISS MARION TR
former Leader Traine

published by
THE UNITED REFORMED CHURCH
GUIDE AND SCOUT FELLOWSHIP

which exists to serve all members and friends of the Guide and Scout Movements who are associated with the United Reformed Church in the United Kingdom. The principal aim of the Fellowship is to equip members better for the understanding and practice of Duty to God, and for the guidance of others into such understanding and practice.

Margaret Nineham (Secretary),
Village, Ashford,

INTRODUCTION

Following the issue of TROOP PRAYERS by the Congregational Scout Fellowship, it was not surprising that requests for a book of PACK PRAYERS should follow. This collection of prayers is offered to all who may find them helpful in leading Cub Scouts in prayer.

Leaders not accustomed to praying aloud should not declaim or pronounce the words in solemn tone nor in any sort of 'put on' voice. Speak clearly and slowly with appropriate pauses, and as you would to a very dear friend. Lead up to prayers with a quiet game or yarn. Let it become a tradition of the Pack that there is definitely no fooling about at prayer time. All adults present should take part as well as the boys.

Choose, and if possible read the prayer aloud, before the Pack Meeting. Ensure that it will appropriately
w the occasion or arise out of the
d, nevertheless, to ch
xtemporise

Persevere with the responsive prayers until your Pack can do them well, with every member speaking out clearly. It will be found helpful for at least every Sixer to have his own copy of PACK PRAYERS.

I am grateful to those friends, at home and abroad, who have sent me prayers. I wish to record thanks to the Rev John M Sutcliffe for permission to adapt some of his TROOP PRAYERS; for his patient reading of the prayers I have written and collected; and for his helpful suggestions. My thanks are due also to Mr Neil Davis who prepared the copy for the printer and who designed the cover.

MARION TREADAWAY

Note: TROOP PRAYERS is no longer obtainable.

THE CUB SCOUT LAW

Let us pray:

O Lord Jesus Christ, who went about caring for others, help us to keep our Cub Scout Law.

Give us strength to do our best always.

Keep us watchful so that we may see where a good turn is needed and, not waiting to be asked, be ready at once to do it.

Help us to think, day by day, how we may be helpful and useful:

at home,
at school,
in our Cub Scout Headquarters,
towards elderly people,
towards little children.

O Lord our God, may our Hero and example in usefulness and helpfulness always be Jesus Christ.

Amen.

THE CUB SCOUT PROMISE

linking Cub Scouts across the world

1. Tonight, as we use an Australian Cub prayer, we remember Packs all over the world in which boys are doing their best to keep the same Promise. Some meet on tiny islands in the heat of the Caribbean Sea, and others a long way from any other Pack, like the one in Tennant Creek, Australia, whose nearest Cub Pack is 300 miles away at Alice Springs.

   Let us pray:

   > Help us, O Lord, to serve You day by day,
   > To do our duty and to enjoy our play,
   > To keep our Cub Scout Promise, and to rest
   > Happy that we have tried to do our best.

   (The Pack should be encouraged to learn the above prayer and say it together)

2. Let us pray:

Help us to remember, O Lord, that we are members of the world-wide brotherhood, and that every Cub Scout and Scout has promised to do his best to do his duty to You. Teach us to be worthy, we pray, of the uniform we wear; and help us to make our best better and better in Your service, for the sake of Jesus Christ, our Leader. Amen.

THE CUB SCOUT PROMISE

and what it means to us

1. "I PROMISE"

Let us remember that the words "I promise" mean

"I really will, you can count on me,"

not

"I will if I feel like it."

Let us ask God to help us:

Father God, we know we are Your children,
We want to serve You well,
We want to keep our Cub Scout Promise.
Help us to listen to You;
Help us to be willing and quick to do Your work;
Help us to be friendly;
And help us to thank You every day
for all Your gifts to us. Amen.

2. "THAT I WILL DO MY BEST"

We were made by God and He knows what is our best. If we try very hard He will know. If we fail, we must try again and He will help us.

Let us pray:

Father God, You know what is easy and what is hard for each of us, for we are all different. Help us to do our best, and when we fail, help us to try again. Amen.

3. "TO DO MY DUTY TO GOD"

Jesus said "You are My friends if you do what I command you."

Let us pray:

Lord Jesus, we are glad that we can be Your friends. May we be true friends, learning all we can about You. Help us to serve You all our lives. Amen.

4. "AND TO THE QUEEN"

We help the Queen by being the best Cub Scouts that we can; remember that when we sing "God save the Queen" we are really praying for her.

Let us pray:

Father God, we ask Your blessing upon Elizabeth, our Queen, in all the work she does for our country and for the Commonwealth to which we belong. Be with her on her long journeys and bless her Family. May her statesmen pass wise laws and may we, as Cub Scouts, always do our best to obey them. Amen.

5. "TO HELP OTHER PEOPLE AND TO KEEP THE CUB SCOUT LAW."

Jesus said, "Anything you did for one of my brothers here, you did for Me."

Let us pray:

Father God, Your son Jesus went about doing good. Help us day by day to try to be like Him; to be ready to do our best; to do good turns to others; and so make the world around us a better place. We want to do this for You, for Jesus' sake. Amen.

INVESTITURE

1. Let us pray:

Father of all we pray a special blessing for .... who has this day joined our Pack in the world-wide brotherhood of Scouts:

Help him to do his best to keep the Promise
wherever he may be,
whatever he may be doing,
and whatever he may be thinking or
feeling.

Help us all to help him by what we do and say, and by showing that he is really our friend.

ALL Thank You, Father God, for letting us all be real Cub Scouts.

(Alter "he" and "has" to "they" and "have" when appropriate)

2. Let us pray:

Thank You, Father God, for making it possible for .... to join our Pack and the world-wide brotherhood of Scouts. Now that he has made his Promise, help us all to help him to keep it. Especially may we try to learn all we can about Jesus, whom You sent to show us how to live. Then may we try very hard to live like Him.

ALL Show us please God, how we can best help others, and give us strength to keep our Promise. Amen.

AWARDS

(Arrows, Sixer appointment, etc.)

Before reading, delete in pencil the words not required and add others.

Let us pray:

Father God, we give our praise and thanks to You;
for You are our friend.

You love us and look after us,

And nothing happens without You noticing.

So we know You are happy that some/one of us have/has earned our/his .... badge.

Do please keep on being helpful to us all. Amen.

GOING UP

Let us pray:

Our Loving Father, we are always in Your care, and we know that You will continue to be with .... as he goes up from the Pack to the Troop. Please help him as he learns new and more difficult things, and bless his new friends and Leaders. Amen.

(Alter "he" to "they" when appropriate.)

OUR FOUNDER

Let us pray:

We thank You, Father God, for the help that comes to us through Scouting. We thank You for our Founder, Lord Baden-Powell and for all who follow his lead. Bless the Leaders of our Movement, both those who work with men and women and those who work with boys. May they help us all to be true Scouts and sons of God. Amen.

A BIRTHDAY

Let us pray:

Father God, who made us and gave us all that we have, we ask Your special blessing on this, ...'s birthday. We thank You for the past year of happy days in which You have helped him to grow in body, in mind and in spirit. Be with him now as he begins another year of his life. Help him to rely on Your help at all times by following in the way of Jesus. Amen.

A PACK BIRTHDAY

Let us pray:

Please God, bless this Pack especially this day, when we are celebrating our .... birthday. Bless all who have been members of the Pack in the past, wherever they are. May they always remember their Cub Scout Promise and do their best to serve You as we are trying to do. Bless all of us who are now in the Pack, and help us to make ourselves worthy members, not only of this Group, the ...., but also of the whole world-wide brotherhood of Scouts. Amen.

FOR A CUB SCOUT OR SCOUTER

absent through illness or other trouble

Let us pray:

We thank You, Father God, for this happy day and we specially ask You to bless and look after .... Keep him safe and happy, we pray, with the knowledge that You are near him at all times. Bless all sick people, and forgive us that we are often without thought for the troubles of others. We do thank You for our many blessings, but above all for Your love and care for each one of us. Amen.

(Alter "him" to "her" or "them" when appropriate)

FOR CUB SCOUTING

Let us pray:

We thank You, Father God, for our Cub Scouting and all that it means to us. We thank You for the fun and the things we learn to do; the chances of helping other people which is our way of trying to serve You. Make us better able to do our good turn, we pray, and give us, each week, a better understanding of our Promise, for Jesus' sake. Amen.

FOLLOWING A HANDCRAFTS EVENING

1. Let us pray:

   Thank You, Father, for the ideas we had, for the use of our hands, for the materials and tools with which we worked. It was great fun. Thank You, Father. Amen.

2. Let us pray:

   Father God, You are the maker and doer of the most exciting things. We are glad that, because we are Your children, we also have such exciting things to do. Amen.

3. *It is suggested that only the appropriate lines of the following prayer are used, or if other material is used, new lines could be composed. The Pack should be told that the response after each line is "We thank You, Father God".*

   Let us pray:

   For wood and nails, for hammer and saw,

ALL We thank You, Father God.

LEADER For paper and card, for clips and pins,

ALL We thank You, Father God.

LEADER For paste and paint, for sand and clay,
ALL We thank You, Father God.
LEADER For feathers and cork, for plaster and wire,
ALL We thank You, Father God.
LEADER For magnets and tacks, for twigs and wax,
ALL We thank You, Father God.
LEADER For wool and cloth, for needle and thread,
ALL We thank You, Father God.
LEADER For flour and water, for ovens and pans,
ALL We thank You, Father God.
LEADER For all things we can make or do,
ALL We thank You, Father God.

NEW SCHOOL TERM

At the beginning of this new term, let us offer it to God in our prayers.

Let us pray:

Father God, we bring before You the work that we shall do during this school term, especially that which we find difficult. Give us strength to overcome those weak moments when we are content to do less than our best, and help us to do all work as a gift we are offering to You. We remember before You our school friends and teachers. Help us to grow in friendship and obedience, through Jesus Christ our Lord. Amen.

HOLIDAYS

Let us think about:

> the time we spend at home in company with our family and friends;
> the freedom to follow a hobby, to cycle, to fish, to collect things, and to play games;
> the excitement of going away, the wonder of the countryside, and the thrill of new interests;
> those who work to make our holidays enjoyable;
> and the Churches which welcome us as visitors.

Let us pray:

Father God, we thank You for our holidays. Teach us to think of them as our chance to fit ourselves for whatever lies ahead.

Let us remember all those who are unable to enjoy a holiday: those who are ill in body or mind; the poor; the refugee. Father God, in Your mercy, give them other things instead; through Jesus Christ our Lord.

Amen.

ABOUT JESUS

1. *The Pack should be told that the response after each line is "Thanks be to God".*

   Let us pray:

   Jesus was loyal to God, His Father.

ALL Thanks be to God.

LEADER Jesus was loyal to His fellow men.

ALL Thanks be to God.

LEADER Jesus stood out against what was wrong.

ALL Thanks be to God.

LEADER Jesus did not run away from death.

ALL Thanks be to God.

LEADER Jesus gave His life for His friends.

ALL Thanks be to God.

LEADER Jesus is our friend. We are His friends if we are loyal.

2. Let us pray:

   For the life of Jesus of Nazareth, we thank You, Father. He spent Himself helping and being a friend to others. He challenged His friends to follow Him, to live dangerously, and to care for others as much as He did. We want to be His friends. Amen.

MORNING PRAYERS

1. Let us pray:

O God, You are the Creator of all things and we thank You this morning for the lovely world in which we live:

for the gold of the sunlight and the dark of the night, and the silver of the moon and the star-scattered sky;
for daylight hours filled with work and games and activity, and for night with rest and sleep;
for the green fields and the grass and the wayside flowers;
for the woods and the tall trees;

ALL We give You thanks, O God.

LEADER We thank You that You have made us as we are:

for hands to work, and feet to walk and run;
for eyes to see, and ears to hear;

ALL We give You thanks, O God.

LEADER We thank You for all that makes life such fun:

for books to read, and for things to learn;
for growing bigger and wiser, and for

the newness of every day;

ALL We give You thanks, O God.

LEADER Bless us and be with us all through today, and help us to live so well that when the evening comes we may have no regrets, through Jesus Christ our Lord. Amen.

2. Let us pray:

Father, we thank You for the night,
And for the pleasant morning light;
For rest and food and loving care,
And all that makes the day so fair.

3. Let us pray:

Lord, our hearts to You we raise
In songs of thankfulness and praise.
Bless us, Lord, and grant that we
Good and true and brave may be.

4. Let us pray:

Be with us, Lord, all through this day,
And make us good and keep us true;
Help us in all we think and say,
And teach us what we ought to do.

(The prayers at 2, 3 and 4 are suitable for the Pack to learn and say together with Leaders.)

5. Let us pray:

Father God, Who has made all things and made them well, we thank You for all lovely things.

For the world in which we live; for the hills and the sea; for the fields and the open road;

We thank You, O Father.

For the books we like to read; for the songs we like to sing; for the stories we like to hear;

We give You thanks, O Father.

For Jesus, that He was a Boy just as we are; that He had to go to school and learn as we have to do; that He grew bigger and stronger and wiser, just as we do; for the way He loved us and for the way in which He is still with us;

We thank You, O Father.

Be with us all through this day. When we are tempted to do wrong, keep us right. When we are tempted to put less than our best into things, help us to play the game. Be with us all through the day, and bring us to the evening time tired but happy, through Jesus Christ our Lord. Amen.

A PACK HOLIDAY EVENING PRAYER

Let us pray:

Father God, who has brought us in safety and in health to this, the end of another day, forgive us:

for the things we did with a grudge, and the things into which we did not put our best;
for the things we should have done that we did not do, and the things we have done that we should not have done;
Forgive us, Father God;
for any chance we missed of making ourselves wiser and of learning something new;
for any chance we missed of helping someone else;
for any spiteful action;
Forgive us, Father God.

Bless all our friends and all who are dear to us. We thank You for our homes and for all the care we receive in them. Help us when we go back home to be more grateful for the love that surrounds us.

Father God, who made night and day, watch over us as we sleep, that we may sleep in peace and wake tomorrow ready to enjoy a new day. Amen.

At the end of a

PACK HOLIDAY OR OUTING

Let us pray:

Thank You Father for this day, for health which gave us strength to play;

For quite enough to eat and drink, for work which gave the need to think.

May our thoughts be kind and true, good thoughts acceptable to You;

May each task we do each day be done in just Your perfect way;

May we spread Your love about to all we meet, indoors and out.

Thank You for Your loving care which follows us both here and there.

Thank You for this lovely day and bless us on our homeward way.

THANKS AT EVENING

Let us give thanks:

Father God, thank You for all the gifts which have made today and every day so wonderful.

Thank You for books to read, books to make us wise, great stories and picture comics;

Thank You for music of every kind, songs to sing, and instruments to play;

Thank You for plays and films, pictures, and every lovely thing;

Thank You for games to play; for "Cub Scouts", where we can meet and talk and play with others;

Thank You for our schools in which we learn, our homes in which we are loved, our Church in which we worship.

Thanks and praise be to You, for all Your kindness and goodness to us.

Hear this prayer for Your love's sake. Amen.

AN EVENING PRAYER
For Forgiveness

Let us pray:

Father God, we thank You for all You have given us today.

Forgive us everything we have thought, or said, or done, which may have hurt others and made You sad.

May the things we have learned and all the fun and games we have had, help us to please You more.

May we take happiness into our homes and wherever we go.   Amen.

FORGIVENESS AND HELPFULNESS

A prayer for each member of the Pack to read, or learn, and say.

Father God, forgive me when I am unkind, and help me to forgive those who are unkind to me or treat me unfairly. Keep me ready to help others, even if it means I miss out on something. Please send me chances to do some good every day, and so grow more like Jesus.   Amen.

WHAT WE SAY

Let us pray:

O God, we pray that You will help us to take care what we say:

> that we may never speak the cruel word which is untrue;
> or, being true, is not the whole truth;
> or, being wholly true, is unkind;

May the words of our mouths and the thoughts of our minds be pleasing to You, our Lord, our Friend and our Leader. Amen.

TO DO RIGHT

Let us pray:

O God, You know how hard it often is for us to do right. Help us to fight against the wrong. Help us to be brave when we are afraid; to be cheerful when we are disappointed; to be pleasant when we feel angry or sulky. Help us always to tell the truth, even when it will bring trouble upon ourselves. Father God, You are strong and You are loving. Help us, we pray, for Jesus' sake. Amen.

CONFESSION

1. Let us pray:

Father, we ask forgiveness for everything that is wrong in our lives.

If we have a grouse against anyone,
if we are jealous of somebody,
if we are resentful and bitter about anything:
In the name of Jesus Christ,

ALL Father, forgive us and help us.

LEADER If we have hurt or treated others unfairly:
In the name of Jesus Christ,

ALL Father, forgive us and help us.

LEADER If we have gone back on our word,
or forgotten to keep our Promise;
if we have been dishonest or deceitful:
In the name of Jesus Christ,

ALL Father, forgive us and help us.

LEADER Help us to see and admit all our faults,
and put things right where we can.
We know You forgive us and love us.
May we be at peace with You and with others
and with ourselves.
Through Jesus Christ our Lord. Amen.

2. Let us pray:

God, our Father, we admit to You that we have sometimes failed to be the real Cub Scouts You meant us to be. When duty has called we have dodged it, and we have defended ourselves with excuses.

We are sorry for our failure, which has hurt ourselves as well as others, and we want to put right what can be put right.

As for those mistakes which cannot be changed we give them up to You. Save us from being worried about them so that we can go forward unafraid, knowing that if we fail, Your help will still come to us.

Through Jesus Christ our Lord. Amen.

ABOUT TOMORROW

Let us pray about tomorrow:

Father God, help us tomorrow:

At school, to keep at our lessons and not to let our thoughts wander;

At games, to play hard and to play fair;

At home, to do our share in the work without grumbling and without having to be asked twice;

In our free time, to enjoy ourselves in such a way that we will do no harm to others or ourselves.

Help us to make tomorrow a happy day for all whom we meet and for ourselves.

This we ask for Jesus' sake. Amen.

MOTHERS' DAY

1. *Ask the boys to say what the word Mum means to them. They could be prompted with: meals made ready, clothes washed, "told off" when naughty, etc.*

Let us pray:

For every good thing that Mum means to us, Father God, we thank You. Amen.

2. Let us pray:

Father God, we know that Jesus was born of Mary, and tonight we remember our mothers. Jesus was held in a mother's arms, and His last thoughts when He hung dying on the Cross, were of concern for her. We thank You, and ask You to help us to help our mothers. Amen.

THE WORLD BEAUTIFUL

Let us pray:

O God our Father, we are grateful that the world is so beautiful and that there is in it so much for us to enjoy.

Thank You for blue skies, for puffy clouds, and for the lovely changing colours of sunrise and sunset; for the green of the fields, the white foam of the sea, and the silvery stars at night. May we always remember that this is Your world. To Your great name we give praise. Amen.

SUPPLICATION

Let us pray:

LEADER Father, as we go to our homes and our school this coming week, we ask You to help us.

SIXER Open our ears.....

LEADER .....to hear what You are saying to us, in the things that happen to us and in the people we meet.

SECOND Open our eyes.....

LEADER .....to see the needs of the people around us.

SIXER Make our hands.....

LEADER .....do our lessons well, and help when help is needed.

SECOND May our words.....

LEADER .....bring comfort, happiness and laughter to others.

SIXER Let our minds.....

LEADER .....discover new truth about You and the world.

PRAISE FOR LIVING THINGS

Let us praise God:

Praise be to You, Lord God, for all Your creatures.
For the animals who give us food and clothes,
milk and butter, wool and fur;
For the pets in our homes,
friendly cats and faithful dogs;
For beautiful birds and delicate butterflies,
silver fishes and quacking ducks;
For the fun of baby animals and the gentleness of
their mothers;
We thank You God, Father of all. Amen.

PETS

Let us pray:

We thank You, Father God, for pets:
For dogs and puppies, full of fun,
For birds out singing in the sun,
For cats that sleep by the cosy fire,
And hamsters biting their cage of wire,
For budgies green and budgies blue,
For the little round bowl with goldfish new;
For furry rabbits and monkeys too,
For sweet, friendly ponies –
Dear God, thank You. Amen.

FOR UNHAPPY PEOPLE

It is suggested that the Leader should choose a number of the following petitions that are appropriate – for example, because of something in the news. The prayer can then be used in various forms on many occasions.

We are fortunate in our homes, our parents, our families, our schools, our Church, our country. Tonight we want to remember those for whom life is not nearly as happy as it is for us.

Let us pray for:

Refugees and others who have no home, no place to call their own;
Coloured people, in lands where coloured people have no rights;
Those who love freedom, in lands where freedom is lost;
Christians, in lands where Christians are badly treated;
Those who are unhappy in their work, badly paid, or made to work in bad conditions;
Those who are treated at home without kindness, and even with cruelty;
Those in a place where it is very difficult to live as a Christian;

The friendless, the lonely, the sad;
Those in hospitals, and in places for those whose minds have lost their reason;
Those in prison and in disgrace.

O God, grant that our own happiness may never make us blind to, and forgetful of, the unhappiness of others.
This we ask for Your love's sake. Amen.

FOR THOSE IN TROUBLE

Let us pray:

O God, bless all the people who are in trouble tonight: those who cannot sleep because they are ill and in pain, or because they are old and lonely, or because they are worried and nervous and anxious.

Bless any who are in danger, especially the children in the war-stricken areas of the world.

Bless those who must work at night:
doctors on call, nurses in hospital and infirmary wards, policemen, and those called out to accidents, fires and shipwrecks.

Bless us now, with a good night's sleep, so that we shall wake tomorrow ready to live strong and true; through Jesus Christ our Lord. Amen.

GENEROSITY OF SPIRIT

Let us pray:

Father God, help us always to believe the best about other people. Help us never to be glad when others go wrong, but to be sorry for them and to try to help them. Teach us when not to speak, and save us from wanting to pass on unkind stories about the people we meet. Make us trustful and generous, like Jesus, our Lord. Amen.

THOUGHTFULNESS

Let us pray:

O God and Father of all men everywhere; help us always to be thoughtful. When there is something we want, teach us to be so thoughtful for others that we may be willing not to have it if it will hurt them. Help us to be thoughtful for fathers and mothers, brothers and sisters, and all our friends. Amen.

FOR THE DEAF

Let us pray:

O God the Father of Jesus, who made the deaf to hear and the dumb to speak, bless all Your deaf children that they may be kept from harm on our busy roads; and that with Your help coming through their families and friends, they may overcome their difficulties. Give us such sympathy with them that our eyes and hands, as well as our lips, may speak the message of love and friendship, in the name of Jesus our Lord. Amen.

FOR ADVENTURERS

Let us pray:

O God, Creator of the Universe, we thank You for scientists, and for those who are brave enough to go out into the unknown vast spaces to find out about other places.

Guard them in their journeys and landings, and make us brave in our small adventures. We remember with thanks that many astronauts were Scouts when they were boys.

FOR COURAGE

Let us pray:

Please God, help us to be brave when we are frightened. Help us to remember that You are near and can give us strength; that You are by our side even when You cannot be seen. Amen.

FOR KINDNESS

Let us pray:

Dear Father God, we pray for kindness. Help us to be thoughtful for the feelings of others, especially those whom we find it hard to like. Help us to remember that we are all Your children.

AFTER A WINTER'S FUN

Let us pray:

Dear God, we thank You for the beauty of winter. For the feel of the cold snow in our fingers, and the warmth of our home; for the freshness in the morning, the ice on the ponds, the delights of all our winter sports, and the cosiness of our beds when the day is done. Amen.

ON BEING KEEN

Let us pray:

O Father God, maker of this wonderful world, help us always to be keen about what we do, whether in work or play, in finding out things for ourselves, or in helping others. May we discover something new every day about the world in which we live, so that when we are grown up, we may be able to play our part and do what You want us to do. Amen.

FOR A SAINT'S DAY

Let us pray:

Teach us, Father, to remember the great example of St.. , who gave up everything to follow You. Help us also to be brave and loyal about the small everyday things that come our way, so that we may be ready and able to do the big things if they should come. Keep our eyes sharp for the chance to serve You, our ears open to hear any call for help, and our hearts brave because of the leadership and friendship of our Lord, Jesus Christ.

Amen.

ADVENT

The Christian year begins with the Advent season, which is the period including the four Sundays before Christmas, when we think of God coming into the world in Jesus, His Son. Jesus was born nearly two thousand years ago, but God is always coming into our lives:

in the needs of people who want help,
in the loneliness or shyness of someone wanting friendship,
in the people we meet wanting a cheerful greeting.

Let us pray:

that we shall let the spirit of Jesus enter into our lives;
that the door of our lives shall not be closed like the unwelcoming inn at Bethlehem;
that we shall be ready to show friendliness and do His will, day by day. Amen.

CHRISTMAS

1. Let us pray:

O Jesus, who was born in a refugee stable,

ALL We praise You.

LEADER That You, our God, showed Yourself to us in a boy like ourselves,

ALL We praise You.

LEADER That You, our God, broke into our human world to show Your love to us,

ALL We praise You.

LEADER That You loved us so much that You came to live with us,

ALL We praise You.

LEADER O Lord our God, receive our praise. Make us strong to live in the spirit of Christmas peace and goodwill, not only now at Christmastide but in every day of our lives, through Jesus Christ our Lord. Amen.

2. Let us pray:

We thank You, Father, for the new life that came into the world with Jesus. We thank You, Father, that as His followers, new life is given to us. Help us to live as Jesus did, loving You, loving others, happy, kind and unafraid. Amen.

3. Let us pray:

Father God, at Christmas time we share secrets about the gifts we shall make for our mothers, fathers, relations and friends. We think about the gifts we should like to have ourselves, and we remember that the first Christmas gift of all was Your Baby Jesus, born for us all.

Thank You, dear God. Amen.

NEW YEAR

(First Pack meeting after Christmas)

1. Let us pray:

   We would thank You, Father God, for all the delight and fun of the Christmas holiday; for all the kindness of our fathers, mothers, grandparents, aunts, uncles and friends who help to fill our lives with joy. May we, with Your help, show to them courtesy and thanks for all their concern for us.

   This year has a new number. Help us we pray to remember our Promise to do a good turn to someone each day of this new year so that, as Cub Scouts, we can be known by our deeds as well as by the badge we wear.

   We ask this in the name of Jesus, whose birthday we celebrated at Christmas.

   Amen.

2. Let us pray:

O God, Father and Creator, we thank You for all the joy of the year that has ended; for all the things we have learned, the fun we have had, and the love that has been shown us. Now we go with You into the New Year. Let us feel Your presence, and teach us to depend on Your help. Help us to be more like Jesus Christ in the coming year. Amen.

EASTERTIDE

This is the second great festival of the Christian year, the first being Christmas. Around these two the Christian year circles. The Easter story is found in Matthew 28: 1 – 10; Mark 16: 1 – 8; Luke 24: 1 – 12.

1. Let us remember before God:

   that Jesus was obedient, even though it meant that he was hurt very much;
   that the men and women who wanted to kill Him were very like ourselves;
   that had we been there, we might have joined them;

that Jesus said that anyone who followed Him
might have to suffer;
that many have died for their faith; others
have been put into prison;
others were laughed at, as we might have been.

(Pause)

But out of obedience there comes reward; out of sadness comes rejoicing; out of defeat comes victory .... to all those who believe.

Let us pray:

Gracious God, we thank You that great pain and death was not the end, but that Jesus was brought alive from the tomb, the conqueror of death; that when most people thought He was finished, then You gave Him the victory of eternal life.

Father God, let us rejoice in the glorious victory of Jesus. Amen.

2. Let us pray:

Jesus, we rejoice that You conquered wrongdoing and death, and that You came back to Your friends full of life and love. Help us to remember that You are with each one of us always, and that You can give us the strength to do right and the power to work for You. Amen.

3. Let us pray:

Father,
Life begins again today,
Jesus lives again today.
Father,
Since life begins again today,
Help us to make a new beginning
With Jesus Christ our Lord. Amen.

WHITSUNTIDE

Whit Sunday celebrates the day of Pentecost, the gathering of the first church, fifty days after Easter. It has been called the "Birthday" of the Church. Let us remember how the Holy Spirit came on the first Pentecost-Whitsuntide and gave a fresh and changed life to the waiting disciples. It was just as Jesus had promised. He would not leave them helpless. He would give them his Spirit. *(A Cub Scout might read part of Acts 2 or part of John 14 from verse 15).*

Let us pray:

Father God, we thank You for Your Spirit which is present in the world. We thank You that through Your Spirit we are not left alone. Your Spirit is power, strength, and gentleness .... Your Spirit is truth, courage, and beauty ....

Come Holy Spirit and dwell in each of us. Amen.

HARVEST

At the Harvest Festival we remember that God is the great Creator. As we have gone about the countryside lately, we have seen that the harvest is ready and is being gathered in. About us in our homes, on our tables and in our wardrobes, there is a reminder each day of the harvest of many countries.

Let us pray:

LEADER O Lord our God, accept our praise for all Your gifts of nature. We praise You for the harvest of land and sea and air; for all the harvests which enable us to live. Forgive us when we take our food and Your giving for granted.

We remember the many people who are underfed, those who live on one meal a day; those who have few clothes; and those who are homeless.

1st SIXER O Lord, help us not to be mean in our giving to others, for so much has been given to us.

LEADER O Lord, show us how to share our good things, by giving to the work of

Missionaries and to organisations which help refugees, the hungry and homeless.

2nd SIXER O Lord, make us feel we want to give You thanks for all that we receive, for You made the world, and are the giver of life.

ALL Great God we praise You, through Jesus Christ our Lord. Amen.

THE LORD'S PRAYER

This paraphrased version should be read in sections for the whole Pack to repeat after the Leader.

Let us pray:

Our Father in Heaven,
May we honour here on earth
every sign of Your presence,
every act of Your rule,
every item of Your plan,
As it is honoured in heaven.
Give us what we need each day, a day at a time;
Forgive us the wrong we have done, as we forgive others the wrong they have done to us.
Do not bring us to a testing which is beyond our power to withstand.
For You have the power, and the authority,
And the glory is for ever Yours. Amen.

Two prayers for the individual Cub Scout. These will need to be duplicated so that each boy may read from his own copy.

AN ATHLETE'S PRAYER

I thank you, O God, for giving to me a body which is specially fit and strong, and for making me able to use it well.

When I compete with others, help me to play fair; when I win, keep me from boasting; when I lose, keep me from making excuses. Let me not be conceited when I succeed or sulky when I fail.

Help me so to live that I will always have a healthy body and a healthy mind.

This I ask for Your love's sake. Amen.

A CYCLIST'S PRAYER

O God, every time I ride my bike, help me to remember that I must have care, not only for my own life, but also for the lives of others.

Give me patience when progress is slow, so that I may not endanger my own life and the lives of others by taking any chances.

Give me courtesy, so that I shall think of the other road user as well as of myself.

Keep me always alert, with the wisdom to know when it is time to stop.

Help me never to try any stunt which would make me a danger to others, and to do all I can to make life safe on the roads on which I ride.

This I ask for Jesus' sake. Amen.

GRACE AT TABLE

1. Father God, we thank You for Your gift of food. Help us never to be wasteful. Teach us to be thoughtful for others, and to be willing to share your good gifts with all who are hungry, for Jesus' sake. Amen.

2. Dear Father, our meal is before us and it smells and looks good. We are happy and we thank you for it. We think of many children throughout the world who have nothing to eat and very little to drink. Please help men and women to give them what they need every day to go through life. Amen.

3. Let us give praise and thanks to our Father God for all the good gifts we receive. Amen.

4. For these gifts of Yours we thank You, Father,
   and we pray
   That all our deeds may praise You, not merely
   what we say. Amen.

CLOSING PRAYERS AND DISMISSALS

1. Dear Father God, we go to our homes happy because we know that You are with us. Amen.

2. For a life in which there is so much to do;
   For a world in which there is so much to explore;
   We thank You, Father God. Amen.

3. The Grace of the Lord Jesus Christ, the Love of God, and the Fellowship of the Holy Spirit, be with us all, now and evermore. Amen.

4. Lord Jesus, You were a happy man
   Because You loved Your Father so.
   Teach us to live as You did then,
   That we as rich in love may grow. Amen.

5. Guide us Father, all our days, and be as close to us as You were to Jesus. Amen.

6. We believe, O God, that You have a plan for the world, and that we can play a part in it. Your wish is that all men should live together happily as brothers. Fill our hearts with joy and peace which will be catching to all whom we meet next week.

7. Show us, Father God, whom we can help, how we can help, and when we can help. May we not be disappointed if our help passes unnoticed.

8. May God, the giver of hope, fill you with joy and peace because you trust in Him.

9. Go out into the world in peace. Be brave; keep hold of what is good; never pay back wrong for wrong; encourage those who fear, help the weak, give due respect to everyone. Be always joyful; keep up your prayers; give thanks often to God.

INDEX